Animal Helpers Sanctuaries

by Jennifer Keats Curtis with
Karine Aigner, Amanda Byrne, Robert Casserly,
Sansa Collins, Pam Fulk, Lori Gagen, Kelly Grenier,
Willow Hecht, Holly Henry, and Lynda Sugasa

Long ago, wild animals only lived in the wild. If they were hurt or orphaned, there was no one to care for them. Nobody thought about owning one. But today, some people do own wild animals as pets or as part of a performing act. Once the cute, cuddly babies grow into big adults with bigger appetites, their "owners" may find that they cannot afford their "exotic pets." They just do not have enough money or support like big zoos and aquariums.

So, what happens to animals that can't go back to the wild because their "owners" can no longer take care of them and they are too used to people to survive in the wild? Who takes care of them? Where?

Luckily, there are sanctuaries, rescue zoos, and even care farms that rescue these animals and provide safe, permanent homes.

In some states, it is not against the law to keep a wild animal as a pet. But this is never a good idea. Would you want a tiger to nap in your bed? How would you talk your mother into feeding raw meat to this binturong?

People may adopt "exotic pets" because they are so different. Cute while babies, they can grow to be large, dangerous, and wild. They can't be tamed like cats, dogs, and rabbits. They're expensive to keep and can't be released back into the wild. That's why Carolina Tiger Rescue is home to many former exotic pets, like this one.

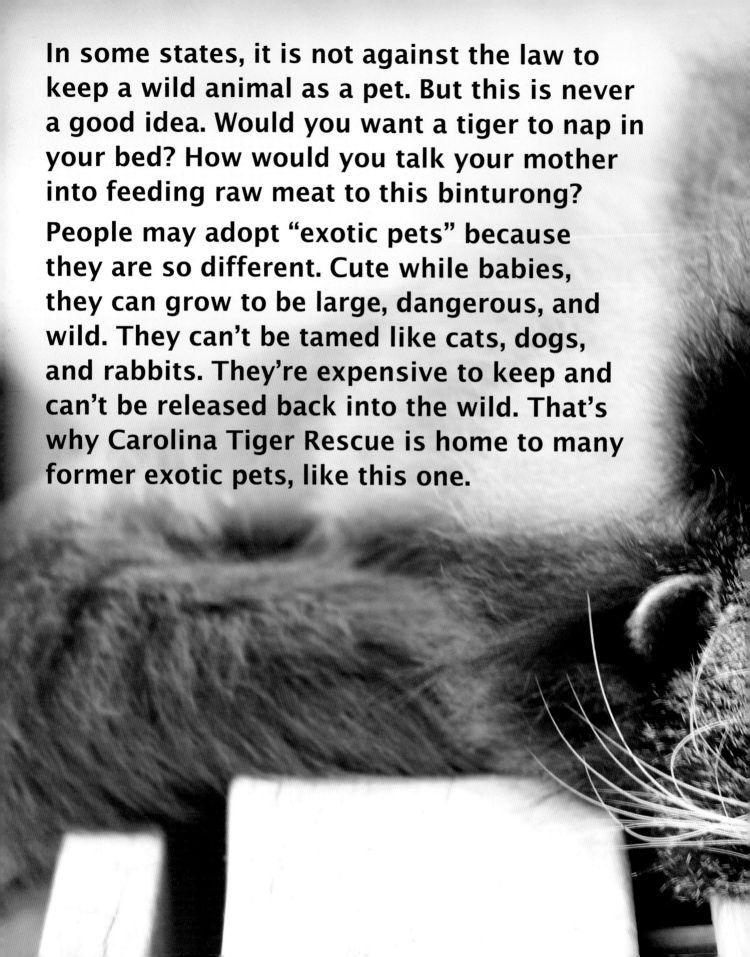

Once sick and starving, tigers Lilly and Titan were rescued by The Wildcat Sanctuary. There, it seems, they fell in love. Today, the happy pair enjoys life together.

Canadian lynx Kiki no longer has
claws. Her teeth are not sharp
because they were filed down.
Fortunately, when her "owner"
became too old to care for her, she
found her forever home at Safe
Haven Rescue Zoo.

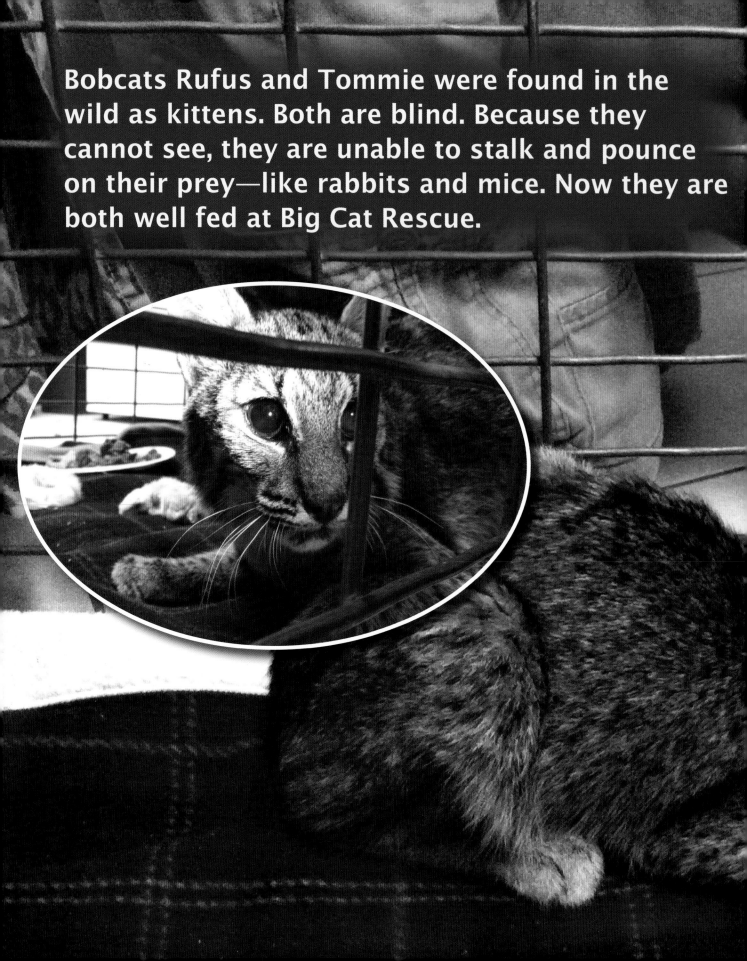

Bobcats Rufus and Tommie were found in the wild as kittens. Both are blind. Because they cannot see, they are unable to stalk and pounce on their prey—like rabbits and mice. Now they are both well fed at Big Cat Rescue.

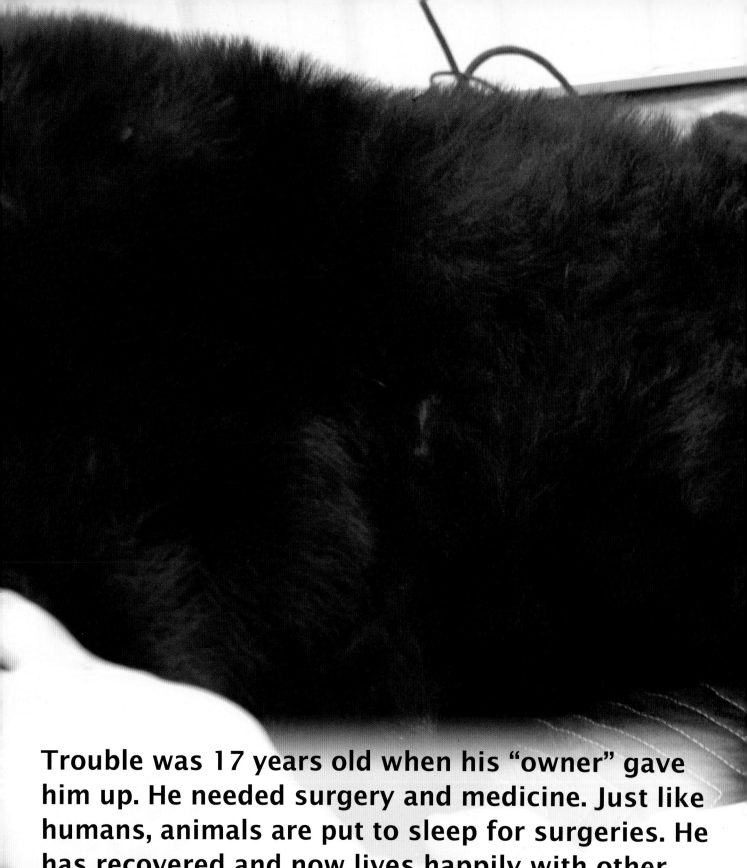

Trouble was 17 years old when his "owner" gave him up. He needed surgery and medicine. Just like humans, animals are put to sleep for surgeries. He has recovered and now lives happily with other bears at the Black Pine Animal Sanctuary.

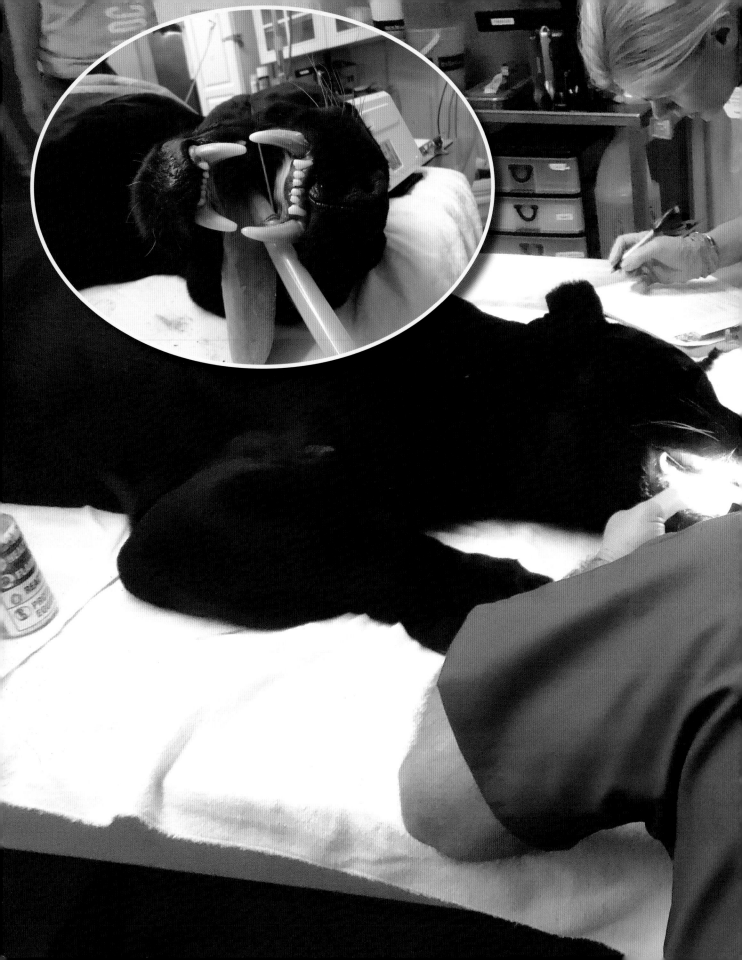

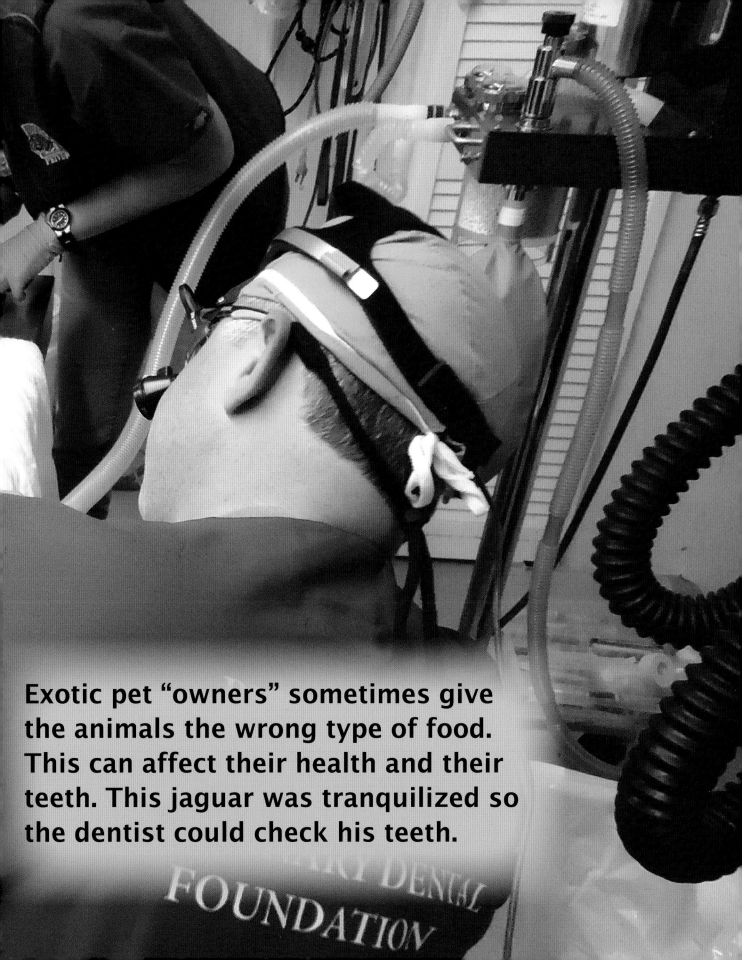

Exotic pet "owners" sometimes give the animals the wrong type of food. This can affect their health and their teeth. This jaguar was tranquilized so the dentist could check his teeth.

FOUNDATION

Emerson the Tiger is clicker trained. His keeper wants to check his tummy for sores. She clicks and holds up her hand so that he will stand on his back legs. When Emerson obeys, the keeper gets a peek and he gets a reward. (He loves chicken.)

In many rescue centers, the animals learn commands but not tricks. This "operant conditioning" is used to reinforce good behavior just as people use clickers to train dogs. The animals are smart and seem to enjoy training. They quickly learn that following commands leads to tasty treats.

Daily care takes place from outside of the enclosures. Veterinarians can squirt flea medication on the back of the tigers' necks, draw blood from the back leg, and offer medicine placed inside meat on a stick.

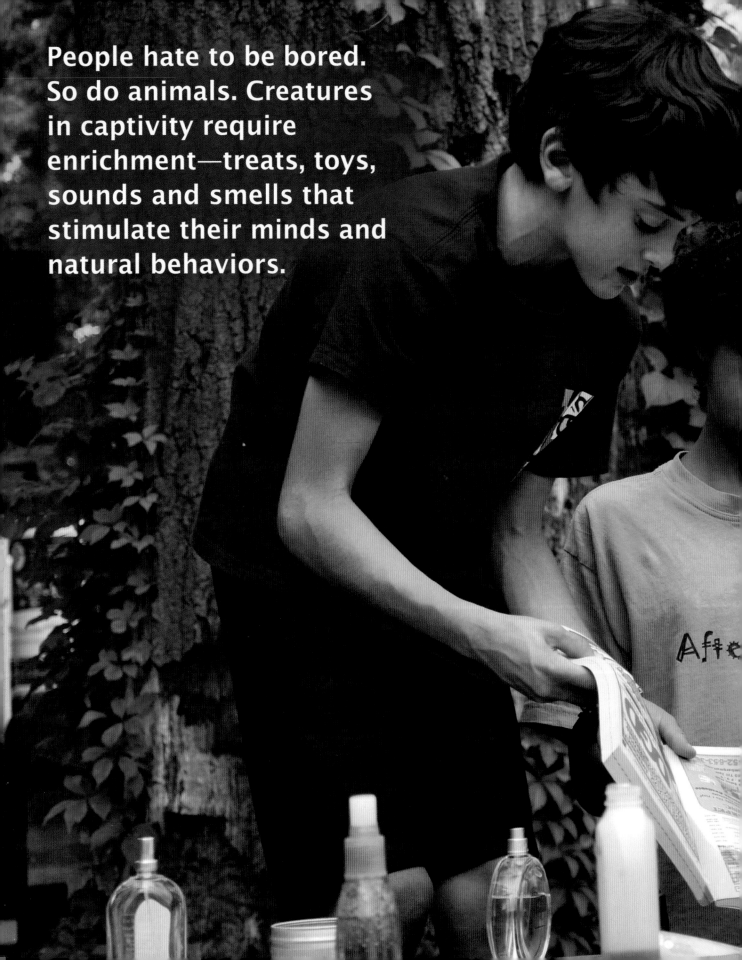

People hate to be bored. So do animals. Creatures in captivity require enrichment—treats, toys, sounds and smells that stimulate their minds and natural behaviors.

Since lions and tigers love different sorts of smells, these summer campers scent toilet paper rolls and phone books with cinnamon, vanilla, and even perfume. The big cats will show how much they love playing with their new toys by batting them and drooling all over them.

To keep track of what the animals most enjoy, volunteers sometimes record their reactions.

Do you think this tiger is enjoying the puppet show?

Farm and companion animals may need new homes, too. When Lisa the Pig reached 700 pounds, her owners couldn't keep her fenced in. Fortunately, Sanctuary One made room. With a high-pitched squeal, this friendly, smart animal now joyfully rolls over for belly rubs.

Care of rescued animals is important but messy. It is expensive to feed these animals. The staffs are small. Volunteers help with jobs like moving and scrubbing cages, cleaning, feeding, scooping poop, and washing water bowls.

For Creative Minds

Domestic Pet, Exotic Animal, or Farm Animal?

Pets are tame. They are companion animals and live with people in houses and on farms. Cats and dogs are well-known pets. Sometimes people keep exotic animals as pets. Even if people keep "exotic animals" from a young age, they still have wild instincts.

Farm animals are raised to produce food (milk, eggs, or meat) or fiber (wool) for humans.

Which animals are pets, exotic animals, or farm animals (livestock)?

Answers: Domestic Pets: cat, dog. Exotic: arctic fox, binturong, Canadian lynx, kinkajou, tiger, wolf. Farm: cow, goat, llama, pig.

Sanctuaries

Animal sanctuaries are "forever homes." They are safe places for animals to live for the rest of their lives. The animals will be cared for and fed but will have enough room to roam so they stay healthy. But how and why do animals get there?

Animals can get hurt or orphaned. They might be hit by cars or they can be injured projecting themselves from predators. Wild animals that are unable to be returned to their native environment may live in rescue zoos, sanctuaries, or education centers.

People who adopt exotic pets don't always realize how big the animals will get or how much they will eat. Even exotic pets that are raised from babies have wild instincts. Those instincts can be dangerous to humans. By the time people realize that they can't care for adult exotic pets, the animals can no longer be released to the wild. These animals often end up at sanctuaries.

Some animals that live in sanctuaries were abused or neglected by their owners.

Circus animals and other "working" animals that can no longer do their jobs are often retired to sanctuaries.

It is expensive to rescue, transport, house, feed, and care for animals, especially big, dangerous animals. Some centers and wild animal orphanages have run out of money. There are only a few places that have the room and can afford to care for these animals.

Centers often cooperate to save money. For example, Safe Haven Recue Zoo, Big Cat Rescue, and the Wildcat Sanctuary have worked together on several rescues, saving lynx, bobcats, lions, and tigers from roadside exhibits, bankrupt wild animal orphanages, and backyard zoos.

Behind the Scenes

Many helpers are needed to care for animals that live in rescue zoos, sanctuaries, or on farms. Veterinarians, caretakers, and volunteers:

Prepare meals, feed and water animals.

Treat and prevent sickness and wounds.

Clean, build, and fix enclosures and cages.

Net, crate, and move animals as needed.

Train animals and record health and behavior.

Enrich animals' lives by offering different activities and foods.

Six animal helper organizations shared their stories. Can you find them on the map? Are any of these places close to where you live?

Big Cat Rescue (Tampa, FL)

Black Pine Animal Sanctuary (Albion, IN)

Carolina Tiger Rescue (Pittsboro, NC)

Safe Haven Rescue Zoo (Imlay, NV)

Sanctuary One at Double Oak Farm (Jacksonville, OR)

The Wildcat Sanctuary (Sandstone, MN)

Animal Enrichment

Wild animals are busy animals. They can't drive to the store to buy food. They have to find their own so they ferret out which plants to eat. Or, they hunt other animals. And, they have to avoid predators who would like to eat them. They need to find safe places to rest and to sleep. But what happens to captive animals, those that live in sanctuaries or on farms? Can they become bored? To keep captive animals' minds and bodies active and healthy, animal helpers provide enrichment. Which of the following do you think might enrich the animals' lives?

Do you like to play ball? So do animals! They chase, kick, and roll on special "Boomer Balls."

Big cats' noses are 14 times "better" than ours are. Campers and volunteers place spices into cardboard boxes and paper bags. They toss these to the cats who will bat them around. Sometimes the cats even kick them like a soccer ball!

Animals like playing with stuffed animals, just as you do.

Do you like to finger paint? Many animals seem to enjoy "paw painting." This tiger seems tired after painting.

Just like domestic cats, big cats like to climb and sit high so they can see what's going on. Most big cat enclosures include tall perches for cats to sit and watch the world go by. Lots of trees make it easy for the big cats to climb.

Sanctuaries provide living areas similar to animals' native environments. Much as he would in the wild, this serval has come out of hiding to pounce on his prey.

Tigers love water; they'll even take bubble baths! This makes it hard to discipline them sometimes. When big cats fight, keepers might spray them in the face with water to separate them. But that doesn't work with tigers because they like it!

Animals are sometimes housed together to keep each other company.

Answers: All are forms of enrichment

Thanks to the following nonprofit organizations for sharing their love of animals with us:

Big Cat Rescue, Tampa, FL: www.bigcatrescue.org
Black Pine Animal Sanctuary, Albion, IN: www.blackpine.org
Carolina Tiger Rescue, Pittsboro, NC: www.carolinatigerrescue.org
Safe Haven Rescue Zoo, Imlay, NV: www.safehavenwildlife.com
Sanctuary One at Double Oak Farm, Jacksonville, OR: www.sanctuaryone.org
The Wildcat Sanctuary, Sandstone, MN: www.wildcatsanctuary.org (cover photo credit)

Library of Congress Cataloging-in-Publication Data

Curtis, Jennifer Keats.
  Sanctuaries / by Jennifer Keats Curtis ; with Karine Aigner [and nine others].
    pages cm. -- (Animal helpers)
  Audience: 4-9.
  Audience: K to grade 3.
  ISBN 978-1-60718-611-3 (English hardcover) -- ISBN 978-1-60718-623-6 (English pbk.) -- ISBN 978-1-60718-635-9 (English ebook (downloadable)) (print) -- ISBN 978-1-60718-659-5 (interactive English/Spanish ebook (web-based)) (print) -- ISBN 978-1-60718-647-2 (Spanish ebook: ayudantes de animales: santuarios (downloadable)) (print) 1. Animal sanctuaries--Juvenile literature. 2. Animal rescue--Juvenile literature. 3. Wildlife refuges--Juvenile literature. I. Aigner, Karine. II. Title.
  QL83.2.C865 2013
  636.08'32--dc23
                          2012039949

Animal Helpers: Sanctuaries: Original Title in English, Ayudantes de animales: los santuarios: Spanish eBook Title , Translated into Spanish by Rosalyna Toth

Books in this series: Animal Helpers: Wildlife Rehabilitators, Animal Helpers: Sanctuaries, Animal Helpers: Zoos (future title), Animal Helpers: Aquariums (future title), Animal Helpers: Raptor Centers (future title)

Lexile Level: 860

Manufactured in China, December 2012
This product conforms to CPSIA 2008
First Printing

Sylvan Dell Publishing
Mt. Pleasant, SC 29464
www.SylvanDellPublishing.com